GEOMETRY IN
ARCHITECTURE

□△○

TEXAS BUILDINGS
YESTERDAY
AND TODAY

GEOMETRY IN

Original edition photography and layout by
MARYANN HEIMSATH

Revised edition photography coordinated by
LISA HARDAWAY

ARCHITECTURE

TEXAS

BUILDINGS

YESTERDAY

AND

TODAY

by CLOVIS HEIMSATH, FAIA

Foreword to the original edition by
LOUIS I. KAHN

UNIVERSITY OF TEXAS PRESS ♦ AUSTIN

PHOTO PAGE II BY MARYANN HEIMSATH
PHOTO PAGE III BY HESTER + HARDAWAY

PHOTOGRAPHERS:

B&V	BLACK & VERNOOY
BB	BRENT BATES PHOTOGRAPHER
BK	BRIAN KORTE
BW	BLACKMON WINTERS
CDS	CHARLES DAVIS SMITH
DF	DAVID FLORY
DL	DAWN LAUREL
EL	EMILY LITTLE
FPC	FORD, POWELL AND CARSON
FW	FRANK WELCH
GB	© 2000 GEORGE BOND PHOTOGRAPHY
H+H	© HESTER + HARDAWAY
H-R	© HICKEY-ROBERTSON PHOTOGRAPHY
IP	IRVING PHILLIPS
JM	JOE MASHBURN
LAKE	DAVID LAKE
LH	LISA HARDAWAY
LWS	LAWRENCE W. SPECK
LYON	MICHAEL LYON
MH	MARYANN HEIMSATH
MH&KB	© MILTON HIME & KEVIN BLACKBURN
ML	© MAX LEVY
MUIR	ROB MUIR
OP	© OVERLAND PARTNERS
PB	© PAUL BARDAGJY
PH	© PAUL HESTER
PTP	© PETER TATA PHOTOGRAPHY
PW	© PAUL WARCHOL
RC	ROBERT COOK
RG	© RICK GARDNER
RGH	© R. GREG HURSLEY
RK	ROBB KENDRICK
RM	RICHARD MOGAS
RP	© RICHARD PAYNE
RS	© REX SPENCER/PHOTOGRAPHER— HOUSTON/LOS ANGELES
TA	© TAFT ARCHITECTS
TH	© TIMOTHY HURSLEY

Requests for permission to reproduce material from this work should be sent to
Permissions, University of Texas Press, P.O. Box 7819, Austin, TX 78713-7819.

∞ The paper used in this book meets the minimum requirements of
ANSI/NISO Z39.48-1992 (R1997) (Permanence of Paper).

LIBRARY OF CONGRESS CATALOGING-IN-PUBLICATION DATA

Heimsath, Clovis.
  Geometry in architecture : Texas buildings yesterday and today / by Clovis
Heimsath ; photography coordinated by Lisa Hardaway.
    p.   cm.
  Rev. ed. of: Pioneer Texas buildings. 1968.
    ISBN 0-292-73145-0 (alk. paper)
  1. Vernacular architecture—Texas—Pictorial works.   2. Geometry in
architecture—Texas—Pictorial works.   I. Title: Texas buildings yesterday and
today.   II. Heimsath, Clovis. Pioneer Texas buildings.   III. Title.
  NA730.T5 H4 2002
  720'.9764—dc21   2001007533

CONTENTS

ABOUT THIS BOOK

THIS BOOK UPDATES AND EXPANDS *Pioneer Texas Buildings: A Geometry Lesson*, published by the University of Texas Press in 1968. Thirty-four years ago it was ahead of its time, for it celebrated the simple geometry of early Texas buildings at a time when they were considered by many to be of no historic significance, and were routinely torn down.

Fortunately the climate of opinion has changed over the last thirty-four years. Not only are the remaining buildings cherished for the heritage they preserve, but also Texas architects continue to design with simple geometry, straightforward structures, and local materials to address today's programs.

It is the realization that the geometry lesson of *Pioneer Texas Buildings* is alive today that led the University of Texas Press to publish an updated edition of the book. In the process of revising the book I have contacted many architects across the state and included their work as an example, today, of the principles of design so clear in the early Texas buildings. While the projects presented are only a small sampling of what has been built by these and many other architects, the reader does not have to guess how a building today would look if it were built in the pioneer Texas tradition: there are photos of current work in the book that answer this question. Lisa Hardaway, of Hester + Hardaway, architectural photographers, has coordinated the acquisition of appropriate photographs of recent work.

The format of the book remains the same. Each section reproduces the original photographs by Maryann Heimsath and simple text of the first edition along with photographs of current work by Texas architects designing in this tradition. The transition is seamless. The continuity in design is broadly interpreted to include a wide range of geometric forms applicable to today's programs and materials.   CLOVIS HEIMSATH

I WOULD LIKE TO ACKNOWLEDGE the people and organizations that made the original *Pioneer Texas Buildings* and this revised edition possible.

Pioneer Texas Buildings, 1968

A summer study grant from Rice University was important in getting the project started. Encouragement and financial help from Miss Nina Cullinan were essential in continuing it.

The Texas Historical Society and local society members, particularly in Fredericksburg and Comfort, were of great help, as were Miss Ima Hogg, Mrs. Hazel Ledbetter of Round Top, Diana and Bill Hobby of Houston, and Mrs. Nancy Negly of San Antonio.

Above all, I want to acknowledge the many hundreds of homeowners throughout the Hill Country who have restored their early Texas homes and who encouraged Maryann and me in documenting them.

Geometry in Architecture, 2002

The expanded format of the book was a formidable undertaking, more than doubling the number of photographs. While the additional photos vastly extend the impact of the book, the active participation of architects across the state was required to locate appropriate projects for inclusion. The intent of the book is a celebration of geometry, not a definitive study, so let me acknowledge the scores of Texas architects building in this tradition beyond those represented here.

Acknowledgment must go as well to architectural photographers across the state, foregoing normal reimbursement for photos in order to make this historic document possible. Particular appreciation is directed to Lisa Hardaway, of Hester + Hardaway, architectural photographers of Fayetteville. Not only did she expertly facilitate the process of photographic acknowledgments; she also suggested architects I would not have known to include, helped in page layout, and found additional historic photos to celebrate the thesis.

CONTRIBUTORS

BUILDING OWNERS: My appreciation goes out to all the building and home owners who agreed to have their projects included in the revised edition.

ARCHITECTS: Natalye Appel + Associates Architects, Inc.; Black & Vernooy, AIA; William T. Cannady; Dick Clark Architecture; Croslin and Associates, Inc.; Curtis & Windham Architects; Robert Emmott;

Ford, Powell and Carson, Inc.; Robert Fowler with Burdette Keeland; Glassman, Shoemake, Maldonado Architects; Good, Fulton & Farrell Architects; Heimsath Architects; Milton Hime; Michael G. Imber Architect; Robert Jackson Architects; Carlos Jiménez; Lake/Flato Architects; Max Levy Architect; Emily Little Architects, Inc.; Joe and Julia Mashburn; Richard Mogas & Associates Architects; Overland Partners, Inc.; Phillips/Wild Design; Rey de la Reza; Rhotenberry Wellen Architects; Shefelman and Nix Architects; Lawrence W. Speck; Lars Stanley Architects; Stern and Bucek Architects; Taft Architects; Charles Tapley; Frank Welch Associates, Inc.; Willis Bricker Cannady; Jim Wilson Architect; Tom Wilson + Associates Architects; John Zemanek.

PHOTOGRAPHERS: Paul Bardagjy; Brent Bates Photographer; Black & Vernooy; George Bond Photography; Robert Cook; David Flory; Ford, Powell and Carson; Rick Gardner; Lisa Hardaway; Maryann Heimsath; Paul Hester; Hester + Hardaway; Hickey-Robertson Photography; Milton Hime & Kevin Blackburn; R. Greg Hursley; Timothy Hursley; Robb Kendrick; Brian Korte; David Lake; Dawn Laurel; Max Levy; Emily Little; Michael Lyon; Joe Mashburn; Richard Mogas; Rob Muir; Overland Partners; Richard Payne; Irving Phillips; Charles Davis Smith; Lawrence W. Speck; Rex Spencer; Taft Architects; Peter Tata Photography; Paul Warchol; Frank Welch; Blackmon Winters.

TO SEE THESE MODEST STRUCTURES and see them again in the mind invokes wonder in what inspires the works of man. If I were asked what I now would choose to be, I would say "to be the creator of the new fairy tales." It is from the sense of the incredible that all man's desire to make and establish comes. The simple structures of shelter seem like the markers of a dominating desire to establish a claim out of the vastness of the land, a place from which to dream of anticipated enterprise, full of the promise of a kingdom where the house or the castle is not yet in the mind.

Without historical records the story of America could come from the primitive desires and inspirations, the feeling of joy, which the endless unexplored land can evoke. The spirit of independence, our unique freedom, the feelings of unmeasured generosity and humble hospitality came from the spirit of the unrestricted spaces of the frontier.

The stone and wood, not bought but found, are used true to the rights one dares to take in gratitude for the gifts of nature. These noble and most ancient materials which in all ages inspired numerous and beautiful variations in the expressions of their orders here were used true to their nature with clarity and economy.

Later the Architect appears, admiring the work of the unschooled men, sensing in their work their integrity and psychological validity. They now stand in silence, yet stir the fairy tale and tell of life.

LOUIS I. KAHN, 1968

EARLY TEXAS BUILDINGS BROUGHT ME BACK TO TEXAS. A hundred times I drove down dusty roads through bleak countryside and discovered again a hundred different moods of homes and towns. A hundred moods sprang up from this remembrance, and I had to come home. We can talk about the geometry of these early Texas buildings, and that is their glory, but it is the poignancy of the environment they create, set in the Hill Country, that is the "why" of this book. It would be so easy to forget that, first and foremost, architecture is a reality; it must be dissected to understand how it is formed, so that it can be seen, so that we can learn to see. But the end, the reason, the adventure is the feeling of it; it is the mood it creates; it is the reality of responding to a man-made form, a man-made space.

Early Texas buildings brought me back to Texas. It took me five years to discover it. As this book grew, it became clear to me that these houses had been speaking to me since I had first known them as a child; they had been telling me something about simplicity, order, geometry, about how Texas was a hundred years ago. I have felt the need to say something about architecture; suddenly, in these houses, I found that it was about them I wanted to speak. This book lets it out; this book lets me go on; this book helps me see architecture in basic terms, and I want it to speak to others. Architecture is a great adventure, and when we see it, when we respond to it, we are richer.

I want these houses to speak out against the sham of current American domestic architecture. The fraud is so appalling, it becomes the aesthetic sin of the age by its very magnitude; that we snug Americans can live in our endless four-square rooms with our endless eight-foot-high ceilings while the outsides say everything stylistically under the sun is a fraud—we want it, so we have it. But it damages our spirit to acknowledge this fraud. Our eyes are dulled to the things of architecture, for they accept window trimming, the memory overlay of decoration, in place of significant form, significant space, or the synthesis of the two. A Polynesian broken-eaves roof has the same stuffings inside as a French Provincial mansard-roof façade, or an Old English façade. We are building townhouses today with a Disneyland disregard for form; no one calls fraud when he sees fake plywood chimneys popped on top of gingerbread roof forms. No one calls fraud about a row of townhouses in alternate styles: one French, one Spanish, one Early American. At least we could have the aesthetic decency to admit that all the townhouses in France were French, in England, English, and in Spain, Spanish. With formal fraud on top of formal fraud, no wonder we have so much trouble seeing architecture; no wonder our eyes are dimmed. And the fraud is institutionalized; each Sunday across the country a Home Building Section appears, calling these stylistic frauds beau-

NOTE: This essay appeared as a postscript in the 1968 edition of *Pioneer Texas Buildings.*

tiful, elegant, classic, and well balanced. A generation is growing up believing only the fraud, believing their parents live in a beautiful home because the paper says that a large, aluminum-windowed, two-carred, interior-bathed, vinyl-floored "Early Colonial" is beautiful.

Do we have a problem? We have a problem.

Let's try to see architecture again. Let's start out again; let's see if our eyes can lead our hearts to a new adventure. It doesn't have terms; it has no style; it is a way of seeing. In a world that wants to be "tuned in" and in an age that wants real experience, don't forget the glory, the reality of architecture.

A building is *space and form.* It is a strange and wonderful duality. It is the only form we experience both inside and out; not even in the cave do we really experience the duality, for we can conceive the space within but not the mountain. Outside, a building is an object which can be seen from a distance, small enough to put in our pocket. If we want to control a building visually, we need only walk away from it; sooner or later it's small enough for our ego and we can stop; we've mastered it. Come closer and we're in trouble; any building begins to grow up to overpower us, blank out the sky, and then all at once the moment of visual truth—we step through! No Alice-in-Wonderland looking glass was ever more exciting than this adventure we experience a thousand times a day. We pass through, space-to-space outside, then space-to-space from outside to inside. We're jaded or it would stop us; we're jaded or the wonder of it would haunt us; we're jaded or the two environments—the one outside we control, the one inside that controls us—would intrigue us. Not many years ago men felt this mystery of entering; through history man has made his entry point impressive; he has given it dignity. To look in or out was an act as worthy; the windows, the holes slashed in this form-giving skin, were gracious in size, decorated to entice the eye. Whatever the style, whatever the material, whatever the age, man will move through space, man will continue the mystery of entering and leaving form. And he'll do it from a five-foot, two-inch-high eye level. He'll walk through space or drive, but the measure of man will be the same as it had been through history. Incredible, it's architecture.

There are really *four* things that architecture does. It creates *interior space* that envelops us. It creates an *exterior object,* the formal husk of the space within. It creates *exterior spaces* by the grouping of objects in space (call them buildings if you must) which leave a space in between. Finally, by superimposed buildings it creates *corporate forms* like the skyline of a city. With these simple things to do, architecture makes our environment. If thoughtfully done, if architecturally done, it enhances our mood. Our environment speaks to us, gives us something of our inner longing to be masters of our world, of our short life, of the incredible endless mystery. Without architecture, without thought, the forms still act on us, but the mood is fragmented, it builds nowhere; it becomes an environmental limbo, as most of our environs are today. Our junkyard of thoughtlessly formed cities and our sloppy countrysides are not wrong unless mediocrity is wrong; they are not evil unless it's evil to deprive man of art; they are not worth changing unless to know something of the power of form is important.

Thus, when you find simply stated geometric truths in houses, set quietly in the pensively rugged countryside of Texas, it is important. Architecture is space/form. It is a space within and an object without. When this inner form and outer form are one-one (the form expresses completely the space within) it's refreshing to say the least! In pioneer Texas buildings all the space is used: If the roof is a shed form, the space inside is a shed form; if the roof outside is a pitch form, the space inside is a pitched-ceiling space. Delightfully, the porches do all sorts of things: they are added forms; they are cut-out voids; they turn corners; they are dog-runs dividing the form into two parts—a thousand variations on the same theme, using interior spaces, exterior porches, and clear, related geometries.

Clusters of these forms make farms or towns. Many of the early towns are around a square, like Gonzales, Halletsville, or Fayetteville. Sometimes the square is immense, as at Castroville, or minute, as at Round Top. Sometimes there is a sequence of squares, as in Anderson. It's not St. Mark's Square, but it's real; it works on you just the same. Sometimes a town hall is dropped into the middle of the square, the space is lost, and the object of the pretentious town hall is so big that you wonder what they had in mind. For me, it's the ribbon of storefronts as in Comfort, Waelder, or Schulenburg that makes the statement for exterior space. These fronts become a wall, a line, often paralleling the train track with a ghost wall on the other side almost too far away to be felt. It's a ribbon space, a passing-through space, and it seems entirely appropriate to Texas, where going through takes more of your time than stopping. You are always going through town. It's the farm that is the cul-de-sac place to stop. In Texas, space is endless; you leave the passed-through town, end at the arrived-at farm. The most wonderful example of this is visiting Lange's Mill outside of Fredericksburg. There is a special magic world behind that farm with the waterfall, the farmhouse, and the space across to the enclosing barns downhill.

We live by moods—a thousand times a day we feel them. Most don't stick and become a part of the fabric; when they do, they become part of our person, our reality. I rather think in an afterlife we will remember them still—if so, would they not be religious? Such a mood I relate to this farm. I felt the mood there keenly and can recall it clearly as a precious remembrance.

Architecture is geometry/structure. All forms have form—sounds simple-minded, but it leads somewhere. Forms must be sorted out and stacked in our minds in order for them to have meaning for us;

rather, in order for us to understand our visual world through the symbol of these forms. Forms must be categorized for survival. Natural forms we can break out easily, partly by what they are not. They are not geometric; geometry gives us mastery over forms, for we can conceive of them, use them, make building blocks out of them. As I write, I'm looking outside at the nongeometric, uncontrollable, "formless" forms of trees. The leaves shift, the light makes patches, the forms recede. Try as I might, I cannot control them. Luckily, I have the view ordered by the geometric square of the window.

Buildings are basic geometries because it is through systems of mathematical order that we transcribe form, that we order our physical environment. To talk about an x-x axis and a y-y axis makes as much sense in the geometry of form as it does in the geometry of electromagnetic fields. Geometry is an ordered projection of our thought patterns; it expresses how we think about the concrete. Love isn't geometric, but science is.

But we have to build buildings that stand up—at least for a while. Geometry and structure become cosponsors of form when the building is unselfconscious and the relationship is one-one. Forms are added together in a simple geometry, and they translate the loads to the ground. All the fine architectural forms we find in brick and stone buildings express this form-structure duality nicely, since a curve is the structural path of a load carried by small members in compression. They aren't the designed arches we pop onto our pseudo-Spanish façades to look round and pretty; they are structural arches that carry the load of the wall. Often, today, we don't need the arches to carry the load (for we have steel to span across lintels; we have wood walls behind the brick to carry the weight of the brick and roof to the ground). Why aren't we using the freedom today, opening the walls as never before? Why not go beyond the structural limitations and find a new reason for ripping through the enclosing skin?

Pioneer buildings in Central Texas are a geometry lesson. The forms are simply put together; there is a clear if uncomplicated structural integrity behind them (in the wood houses it is merely responding to the plainer quality of wood frame construction). These simple geometries are expressive of the space within in a simple one-one way. Yet the buildings relate to the special features of their sites, to settings almost as undisturbed as any in America. The environment is saying something to us, much as it did to men who lived simple lives a hundred years ago. In the book, I have stayed out of the cities, stayed apart from the Spanish influences, although these are important in Texas and carry a strong mood quotient. I have wanted to stay where the problem is a simple one, without a style overlay, without the encrustation of change brought on by time. It is in the predominantly German towns of Central Texas that this kind of architecture says its simple piece over and over again.

How did it happen that we have this treasure? Texas history spells it out, and these houses are there to affirm it.

There is a path running from the Gulf of Mexico to Dallas, with settlements dropped as cut-ants drop leaves along the way. It is in this area that houses are clustered. As inevitable as the geometry of architecture is the geometry of nature and man's response to it. He came from Europe, across a different substance than he could walk on, and so he used a boat—incidentally, it may be the other form we experience as an object and as a space, at least a boat in drydock where we can see all of it; it is rather exciting to think of a boat as a house covered almost halfway by water. A boat is a house on its side so the porch is on top and you must run down into the rooms. Or perhaps a house is a boat set on its side so you can run out. But the tyranny of physical geometry controlled our immigrant arrivals as much as the tyranny of that enclosing skin that separates the inside and the outside of our houses. The best they could do was arrive in Texas by the Gulf. First arrivals were explorers, the historians of newness who left us their names for the mystical thing they did here: La Salle, arriving in Matagorda Bay in 1685, making it all right for German immigrants to come to the same bay in the 1840s, more than 150 years later; Coronado, De Soto, now relegated to automobiles, were the giants in space, the astronauts of another age. I knew an astronaut very well, one who died; did I know La Salle a little bit, or Coronado, or the incredible Franciscan priests who set up shop on this moon of yesterday? Have I ever known the cruel, incredible Hernando Cortez, who tramped over the Aztecs in 1519, a hundred years before the explorers started. Who was Cortez?

Who were the Germans who landed in thousands in the 1840s? I know them, for one of them was named Heimsath. Whatever social, interpersonal tyrannies drove him from Germany—perhaps the dictator Metternich, perhaps the potato famines sweeping Europe in those years—he came, and thousands more. He exchanged an interpersonal tyranny for a natural one. He arrived in Galveston, and then went to Indianola for a trek across Texas, to a land grant somewhere above Fredericksburg. In 1846 he saw his friends die of cholera. In any of the other years he fought Comanches, he heard of bandit raids, he lived with the interpersonal tyrannies of the New World on top of the droughts of Texas.

Before 1836 and Texas independence, Mexico promoted colonies. The most successful were led by Stephen F. Austin and Green C. DeWitt. In 1836 Texas armies defeated Santa Anna in some treacherous coastal plain geography, won independence, and intensified immigration. Read the story of the Adelsverein, a society of German princes set up to properly handle the German immigration and to protect their countrymen in the New World. It tells us why New Braunfels is where it is, and Fredericksburg and many of the other German settlements from the Gulf northward. For sheer incompetence it was unparalleled; yet it got land deeded, it drummed up Texas in Germany, it inspired my forefathers to get out before things in Germany got worse. I would like to keep alive the historical fiction that Central Texas is all German. Actually, only a small portion, say 20 percent, of the immigrants came from Germany, but they came early and in organized lots and they settled their cities first. They helped establish the format of the cities, gave them their names, often German, as New Braunfels, Weimar, Frelsberg, New Ulm, Boerne. Polish settlers and already-Americanized settlers from the other states made up the vast part of the other newcomers. Fortunately, for Texas and for this latter-day look, the economy on the whole was not slave. There were few slaves in this central area, so studying pioneer homes has no problem of social guilt, something I wrestle with in affirming plantation architecture.

Life in Central Texas in the second half of the nineteenth century was isolated, rugged, simple, and hard. The houses reflect the virtue of this life. In our age, jaded by a plethora of forms, by visual stimuli screaming to be heard, it is an experience aesthetically and spiritually to follow again a dusty road, to find again the simple form of pioneer Texas houses. Perhaps twilight is the best time—when a nightly form dismemberment takes place, if our eyes are tuned to see it and our minds can rejoice in discovering. The form of the object, expressing the space within, dissolves little by little into the nature that encompasses it, the nature that encompasses the house, the house that encompasses you—unless you must break through the skin of enclosing form and sit outside on the defined exterior space of the porch, unless you feel the anxiety of the quiet upon you and you must leave the house entirely and stand under the form of the sky, surrounded only by the now no longer amorphous form that is the mountains, and wonder about the stars.

I AM TYPING THIS NEW INTRODUCTION ON MY LAPTOP, sitting on an open porch on the square in Fayetteville, Texas, listening to the rustle of the leaves, noting the people as they pass into Orsaks Cafe, delighted to have this chance to speak again about the magic of Texas vernacular architecture.

Much has transpired in thirty-four years: in my life and career, in architecture in general, and in the influence of *Pioneer Texas Buildings*. Maryann and I have five wonderful children; they were brought up for ten years in this small Czech town, are graduates of this extraordinary small town school (total enrollment 185, kindergarten through twelfth grade), and are well into their exciting lives. We launched a recognized architecture firm and succeeded in producing another architect—Ben Heimsath, who graduated from Columbia University and went on to earn a Master of Architecture from Harvard (where he spent as much time as possible in the Business School to learn how to actually run an architectural firm). Now, Ben and his partner, Richard Calloway, own Heimsath Architects, and Maryann and I work for them!

Since I wrote the introduction (postscript) to the first edition, there have been three positive surprises. First, Texans have increasingly grown in their respect for early Texas buildings. Second, Texas architects have used and evolved the geometry lesson of these buildings in their work. Third, the computer revolution visually defines the geometry of a building in three dimensions. Designers, using computer technology in three dimensions, can more confidently define geometric forms in their designs.

RESPECT FOR ARCHITECTURAL HERITAGE

The first surprise is the change in the climate of opinion in Texas about old buildings. Today anyone tearing down an old structure needs to justify the need to do so. This is a radical change from thirty-four years ago. Statewide examples of the change of attitude about historic buildings include the restoration of the King William and La Villita areas in San Antonio, the Swiss Avenue restoration in Dallas, and the redevelopment of the Montrose and Heights areas in Houston. The list goes on and on. For me the change is personalized by two episodes in Fayetteville, Texas, my rural retreat and pulse-taking city.

There is a historic red brick schoolhouse in Fayetteville, built at the turn of the century and still standing. This doesn't sound like such a big deal unless you understand Fayetteville. A state inspector suggested to the Fayetteville School Board that the building could not be used for classrooms in its present condition. He should have explained that ramps and an elevator were needed if the second floor was to be upgraded to meet disability access standards. The Fayette-ville School Board interpreted the report as a condemnation of the building and was prepared to tear it down. A groundswell of support for the building developed from former students who remembered the building fondly, and they prevailed. It has been saved as a major landmark celebrating Fayetteville's past.

In a similar instance, the Fayetteville Bank purchased an adjacent property, including a small hundred-year-old house, to provide a parking lot for its employees. Thirty-four years ago the house would have been a goner. Today the change in attitude toward our Texas heritage made it difficult for the bank, a good neighbor, to tear it down. Instead, a bank board member bought the house from the bank and moved it to a new location in town. It is part of the surprise of Fayetteville itself, rebuilding its town center, encouraging people to move back to town as a result.

ARCHITECTURE

The second surprise is seeing Texas architecture develop in the last thirty-four years. Much of the best architecture in the state is an evolution of the geometry lesson of *Pioneer Texas Buildings*!

It was with some trepidation that I contacted architects in Texas whose work seemed to express the geometry lesson of *Pioneer Texas Buildings*. I was afraid they would think it was stretching the concept to include their current work in the new edition. To my delight I found that many of the architects were familiar with the original edition and had used it in their practice as a reference. One architect remembered O'Neil Ford, the dean of Texas architecture, bringing the book into the drafting room to inspire this architect, then a draftsman. Another architect told me that his client insisted that he duplicate a stair shown in the book (a photo of the stair is included in the expanded Stair section).

By contacting architects across the state I learned a great deal about the last thirty-four years of Texas architecture. Architects have expanded the geometries used in Texas buildings, while still maintaining the integrity of the forms. Many stunning buildings rely only on interlocking rectangular volumes, without the typical triangular roof form. Others combine rectangular and curved geometries in amazing ways. As I filled out the book with new work, the seamless transition from old and new became clear. Contemporary and traditional are terms that fade away when you read the geometry of these buildings.

It is also apparent as the geometry lesson evolves that there are many scales of geometry used today, from the grand scale of the geometry of structures holding up buildings to the geometric detail of railings and sun screens. The geometry lesson of *Pioneer Texas*

Buildings is not only alive and well today but has blossomed in many dimensions.

COMPUTER TECHNOLOGY

The third surprise is the computer and what it can do to show the geometry of buildings in three dimensions. Thirty-four years ago a computer was an expensive and somewhat bizarre instrument. Special rooms built with double floors and insulation to maintain a constant temperature were designed for these extremely expensive machines, and draftsmen were sent away for weeks to learn how to use them. What a contrast to today, when the staff at Heimsath Architects is networked to a server, working in two dimensions and three dimensions interchangeably.

With the computer the architect can see a building before it is built. I can remember spending half a day laying out one perspective. If the owner wanted a different view, it meant another half-day before I could return with the drawing. Now I can develop a three-dimensional model of the building and instantly move around and through it. The importance of this change in design cannot be overstated. We can see the whole building and make changes to improve it before construction begins.

There are other exciting developments. In developing the extraordinary double-curvature splayed roofs and walls at Bilbao, the architect was evolving a geometry that could scarcely be drawn using traditional techniques. I remember reading about Le Corbusier developing molded roof forms for the Paris pavilion in the 1940s. He was forced to build up sand to the form he wanted and then use the sand as forms for the reinforced concrete roof.

In 1958 I studied curvilinear forms in architecture for a Fulbright thesis in Italy. I was able to define the geometries of basic curved forms by building cardboard models and slicing the curved forms into many planes. Today it is not only possible to draw double curvature (that is, curves that go in two directions at once), but it is possible for the architect to send the computer analysis directly to the subcontractor who will use the same computer images to construct the forms. When the cost of such construction becomes economical, it will offer architects the ability to expand the geometry of buildings even further.

In the last analysis the geometry lesson of *Geometry in Architecture* is a base for architecture. As opportunities for change increase, it is important to return again to such a base, where the geometry is clear, the structure has a one-one relationship of outside to inside, and the materials are locally available.

Change will occur, but people will continue to be drawn to central Texas and the magic of the pioneer Texas buildings.

MH

GEOMETRY YESTERDAY

Early Texas architecture is a
geometry lesson.

All things have form.

Natural forms

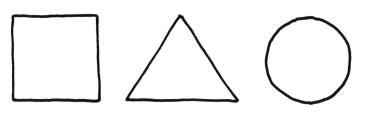

Geometric forms

Put two or three simple geometric forms together and see what happens.

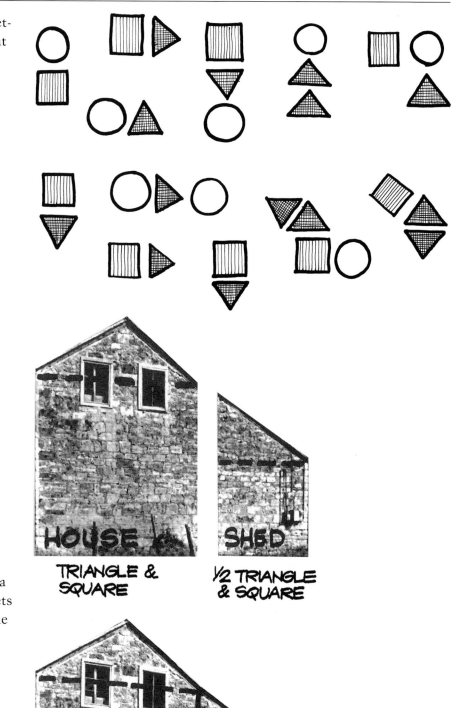

TRIANGLE & SQUARE

½ TRIANGLE & SQUARE

TWO SIMPLE FORMS = ONE COMPOUND FORM

Two forms put together make a compound form. The eye forgets the line in between. It reads the two forms together.

Put a house and shed together. See how it works.

COMPOUND FORM

MH

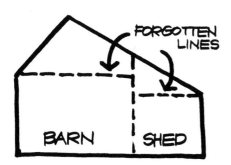

Or add a barn and shed,

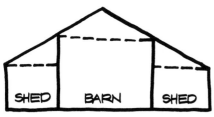

or add a barn and two sheds,

or subtract a porch from a house.

Think big!

Geometry is three dimensional, and so is architecture.

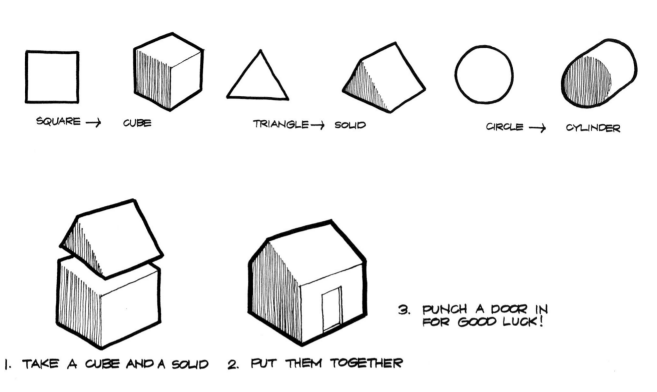

SQUARE → CUBE TRIANGLE → SOLID CIRCLE → CYLINDER

1. TAKE A CUBE AND A SOLID 2. PUT THEM TOGETHER 3. PUNCH A DOOR IN FOR GOOD LUCK!

The "Basic"

The building formed is the early Texas "basic." Things are added or subtracted, but the friendly "basic" always remains —just a cube with a triangular solid on top.

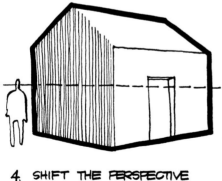

4. SHIFT THE PERSPECTIVE TO EYE LEVEL

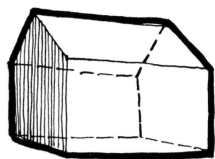

The "basic" again

The "basic" with a shed volume added

All buildings are made up of solids and voids. The solid is the mass of the building; the void is the open part of the building. Windows and doors punched into the mass of a building are voids. An open porch, covered only by a roof but with no sides, is also a void. Early Texas buildings are composed first by simple geometries stacked together, second by solids and voids.

See how these ideas explain the house shown here.

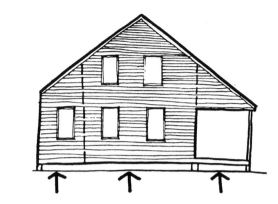

The house is a "basic" with two sheds, one a solid, one a void. Punched in the solid are three additional voids, two windows and a door. With these ideas the house is completely defined.

Voids are two-dimensional (holes in a plane, such as windows and doors).

Voids are also three-dimensional (holes in the cubic volume of the building).

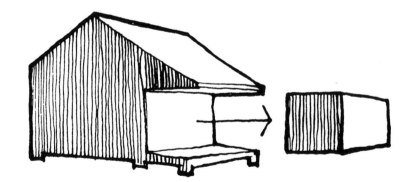

All the parts have a job to do.
In this barn the "basic" is surrounded by sheds. In the barn
above, voids open into the center
volume or into the sheds.

How did these forms get that way?

They needed to have this shape to get the job done. Early Texas houses, barns, and sheds are completely functional. Form follows function and nothing is left over.

MH

MH

MH

MH

MH

MH

These early Texas buildings
can be found as a part of the
geometry of the landscape.

Salado on Route 36 near
Caldwell

Route 16 near Kerrville

Round Top

Route 237—Round Top

Route 16 between Fredericksburg
and Kerrville

Route 1457 near Round Top

Route 237—Carmine

Honey Creek, on Route 46—
Camp Verde

GEOMETRY TODAY

Texas architects today continue the tradition of building with clear geometry, suggesting that the geometry lesson of *Pioneer Texas Buildings* is as valid today as it was yesterday. The forms of buildings are more varied today, as additional geometric relationships are explored.

H+H CARLOS JIMÉNEZ

LAKE/FLATO ARCHITECTS, INC.

LAKE/FLATO ARCHITECTS, INC.

WILLIAM F. STERN ASSOCIATES

FRANK WELCH ASSOCIATES, INC.

Traditional and *contemporary* are terms that mean little when geometry is being considered. Pioneer Texas builders used geometric forms yesterday to provide shelter, and architects use geometric forms today in solving current design programs.

CROSLIN AND ASSOCIATES, INC.

LAKE/FLATO ARCHITECTS, INC.

H+H

FRANK WELCH ASSOCIATES, INC.

PH

CARLOS JIMÉNEZ

H+H

FRANK WELCH ASSOCIATES, INC.

CARLOS JIMÉNEZ

PH

LAWRENCE W. SPECK

RGH

FW FRANK WELCH ASSOCIATES, INC.

RG FORD, POWELL AND CARSON, INC.

A TRIANGULAR SOLID

BECOMES A CUBE WHEN THE POINTS COME TOGETHER

WITH ONLY COLUMNS BENEATH IT IS A PAVILION

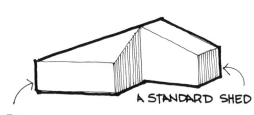

A DIAGONAL SHED   A STANDARD SHED

FRANK WELCH ASSOCIATES, INC.

RHOTENBERRY WELLEN ARCHITECTS

FRANK WELCH ASSOCIATES, INC.

Today's buildings are often more complex and often require more complex geometric forms. Architects interlock rectilinear volumes, triangular volumes, and in some cases circular volumes to solve the needs of a building.

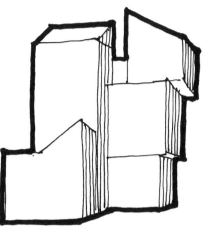

BUILDINGS CAN BE STACKED UP LIKE BUILDING BLOCKS

H+H   NATALYE APPEL + ASSOCIATES ARCHITECTS, INC.

ML   MAX LEVY ARCHITECT

Some building geometry is based on triangular forms.

More examples of geometric
forms placed together. Note that
solids and voids and a variety of
materials are employed.

HEIMSATH ARCHITECTS

TAFT ARCHITECTS

ROBERT JACKSON ARCHITECTS

RK

PHILLIPS/WILD DESIGN

MUIR

MILTON HIME

HEIMSATH ARCHITECTS

HEIMSATH ARCHITECTS

HEIMSATH ARCHITECTS

Geometric form can be used to define a single plane, as seen in the photo below. (See pioneer Texas storefronts on pages 148–153).

Geometric forms can repeat, establishing a rhythm of building elements, as seen in the buildings to the right.

PH   CISTERN

A functional water tank from pioneer Texas times is based on the geometry of a cylinder. Programs today use the geometry of the cylinder, often combined with other forms, to produce a building that works.

PH
HISTORIC BUILDING

BK   LAKE/FLATO ARCHITECTS, INC.

A CIRCLE 〇

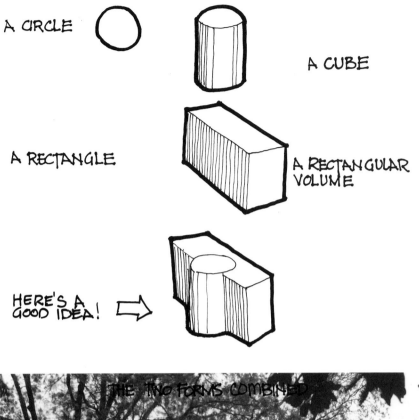

A CUBE

A RECTANGLE

A RECTANGULAR VOLUME

HERE'S A GOOD IDEA! ⟹

THE TWO FORMS COMBINED

Great geometric variety is possible with cylinders combined with rectilinear volumes.

H+H

GLASSMAN, SHOEMAKE, MALDONADO ARCHITECTS

H+H

GLASSMAN, SHOEMAKE, MALDONADO ARCHITECTS

33

FRANK WELCH ASSOCIATES, INC.

NATALYE APPEL + ASSOCIATES ARCHITECTS, INC

HEIMSATH ARCHITECTS

Geometric forms, whether recti-linear or curved, do many things. In the building to the right, the forms defined the front face of the building.

WILLIAM F. STERN ASSOCIATES

34

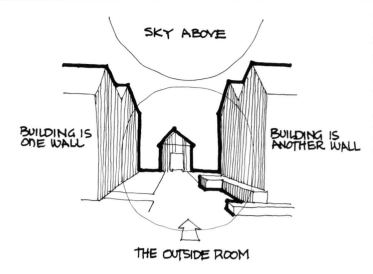

SKY ABOVE

BUILDING IS ONE WALL

BUILDING IS ANOTHER WALL

THE OUTSIDE ROOM

In the buildings below, the geometric forms on both sides define a space outside the building, as if the outside were a room. The outside space becomes an outside room . . . without a roof. It is amazing what geometry can do!

PH   WILLIAM F. STERN ASSOCIATES

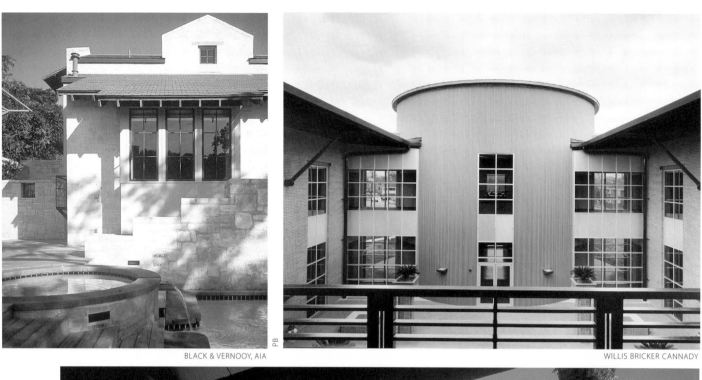

BLACK & VERNOOY, AIA

WILLIS BRICKER CANNADY

LAKE/FLATO ARCHITECTS, INC.

H+H

FRANK WELCH ASSOCIATES, INC.

B&V

BLACK & VERNOOY, AIA

H+H

JOHN ZEMANEK

DICK CLARK ARCHITECTURE   PB

CARLOS JIMÉNEZ   H+H

LAKE/FLATO ARCHITECTS, INC.   LYON

PORCHES YESTERDAY

It is hot in Texas. The early Texas house has a porch of some kind. Porches are either integral, that is, part of the main volume, or added, with two volumes connected.

INTEGRAL PORCH

ADDED PORCH

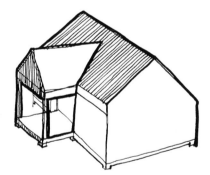

INTEGRAL PORCHES

Two-story porches give second-floor rooms shade and views to both front and rear. They have much greater volume and are more difficult to build than cut-out porches.

CUT-OUT PORCH

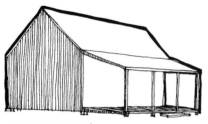

SHED PORCH

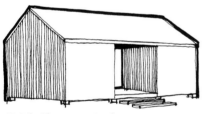

DOG-RUN PORCH

2-STORY PORCH

1-STORY CUT-OUT PORCH

2-STORY PORCH

Cut-out porch

A cut-out porch has a low, low room above.

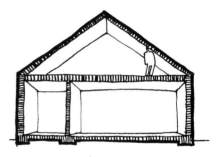

Push up the center section so that people can stand up.

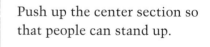

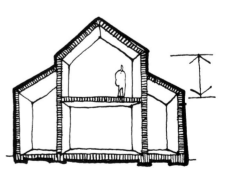

The cut-out porch becomes a shed porch.

More shed porches

Another shed porch

Shed roofs turn a corner.

Houses with porches in the middle are called dog-run houses. The breeze circulates through the house. In a sense it's two houses under one roof. When positioned to receive the prevailing winds, the house is as cool as it can be on a Texas summer day.

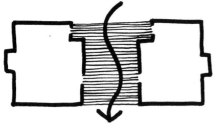

A two-story dog-run porch

MH

A two-story porch with an added porch surrounding the central building

MH

The two-story porch "classic"

MH

MH

A second-story porch hung off the building

ADDED PORCHES

Two forms at right angles to each other are pushed together to make the cross-axis porch.

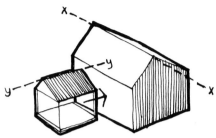

Two forms parallel to each other make a lateral porch.

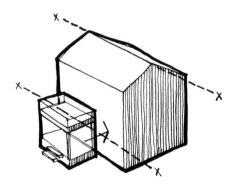

MH

MH

PORCHES TODAY

Even with air conditioning it is hot in Texas.

Porches today are outdoor rooms with a roof above. The roof is often no more than open rafters to provide shade, for even with air conditioning there is a need to shade the house. Note how similar the porches seem, with traditional or contemporary details.

H+H

LAKE/FLATO ARCHITECTS, INC.

TA

TAFT ARCHITECTS

MH

HEIMSATH ARCHITECTS

MICHAEL G. IMBER ARCHITECT

TAFT ARCHITECTS

BLACK & VERNOOY, AIA   B&V

Porches today are designed much as porches were designed in pioneer Texas buildings. The sun is the same, and the use of the porch is the same. The porch remains an integral way of shading the building and making it fun to sit outdoors.

RICHARD MOGAS AND ASSOCIATES ARCHITECTS

MICHAEL G. IMBER ARCHITECT

53

TOM WILSON + ASSOCIATES ARCHITECTS   H-R

EMILY LITTLE ARCHITECTS, INC.

On a porch it is possible to expose the structure and in so doing add a repetitive rhythm to the composition. The roof members are a critical part of the design, for they hold the roof up!

LARS STANLEY H+H

LAKE/FLATO ARCHITECTS, INC.

More porches in today's houses.
Note the porches wrapping
around the house following the
pioneer Texas tradition.

WILLIAM T. CANNADY PH

LAKE/FLATO ARCHITECTS, INC.

FORD, POWELL AND CARSON, INC.

MAX LEVY ARCHITECT CDS

EMILY LITTLE ARCHITECTS, INC. DF

RHOTENBERRY WELLEN ARCHITECTS H+H

WILLIAM F. STERN ASSOCIATES

In geometry a porch is really a shed. Put two sheds together and you have a pavilion or a carport.

A PORCH WITHOUT THE HOUSE

ANOTHER PORCH WITHOUT THE HOUSE

PUT THEM TOGETHER AND YOU HAVE A CARPORT OR OUTDOOR ROOM

LAWRENCE W. SPECK

WILLIAM F. STERN ASSOCIATES

H+H

RHOTENBERRY WELLEN ARCHITECTS

ML   MAX LEVY ARCHITECTS

Then there is the possibility of
making the whole house a porch,
a porch that goes on and on to
provide space for various family
activities.

JOE & JULIA MASHBURN

JOE & JULIA MASHBURN

JOE & JULIA MASHBURN

STAIRS

STAIRS YESTERDAY

Geometrically an inclined plane, most stairs are inside the house.
They lead to the triangular volume above.

65

MH

MH

Some stairs are outside the house, either at the end of the Texas "basic" or within the porch. These stairs become part of early Texas geometry.

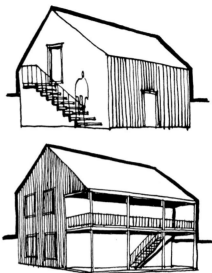

Outside stairs lead to a very low space above, used for storage or sleeping.

The main floor is half a level above the street; a basement is below.

This is an early Texas "split level."

Why does the early Texas house have outside stairs? They save valuable space inside and allow two families to use the same house. A covered porch stair provides some rain protection.

GB   MICHAEL G. IMBER ARCHITECT

RM   RICHARD MOGAS

STAIRS TODAY

In the photo below the owner wanted a stair right out of the original edition of *Pioneer Texas Buildings,* and that is what the architect delivered.

The stairs in the buildings to the left and above also recall pioneer Texas buildings, with an outside stair to the second floor.

WILLIAM T. CANNADY

Stairs are a diagonal with rich
design opportunities. Note, for
example, that each step can be
expressed or all of their edges
can be covered with a diagonal
piece of wood (a stringer). Note
how the posts holding the stairs
are themselves geometric and in
the case at right envelop a bench.
(Like an outside room inside?)

TOM WILSON + ASSOCIATES ARCHITECTS

CURTIS & WINDHAM ARCHITECTS

GLASSMAN, SHOEMAKE, MALDONADO ARCHITECTS

The diagonal geometry of stairs becomes a major design element as a part of an overall geometric volume. (Note that there are two scales in these photos—the large scale of the space itself and the smaller scale of the stairs within the space.) Various scales make a space come alive by articulating the parts.

WILLIAM F. STERN ASSOCIATES

HEIMSATH ARCHITECTS

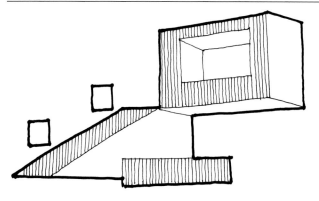

LOTS OF GEOMETRY MAKES AN INTERIOR SPACE

Geometry is used to define interior space and the way light enters. Note that light enters between the geometric forms and makes the geometry glow.

CHIMNEYS YESTERDAY

Texas can be very cold. The chimney shape covers the wide "fire box" below and the narrow flue above.

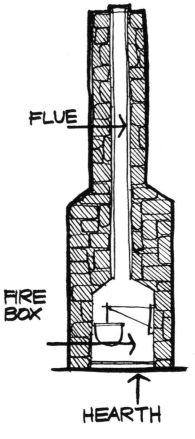

FLUE

FIRE BOX

HEARTH

All the form of a chimney and fireplace is functional.

Outside

Inside

CHIMNEYS TODAY

The vertical form of a chimney is a design element today as it was in pioneer Texas buildings.

GB   MICHAEL G. IMBER ARCHITECT

RM

RICHARD MOGAS

FRANK WELCH ASSOCIATES, INC.   H+H

The chimney is a major vertical design element today as it was yesterday. Note that the chimney may be the same material as the wall or a different material to highlight the change in geometry.

MAX LEVY ARCHITECT   ML

In these buildings note how the vertical geometry of the chimney becomes part of the rhythm of the composition.

RHOTENBERRY WELLEN ARCHITECTS

RHOTENBERRY WELLEN ARCHITECTS

Fireplaces are a focal point in these buildings.

The geometric contrast between inside and outside is magnified in the building below, a studio built around the fireplace.

Note that some of the fireplaces are symmetrical and some asymmetrical, but in every case they are important to the space.

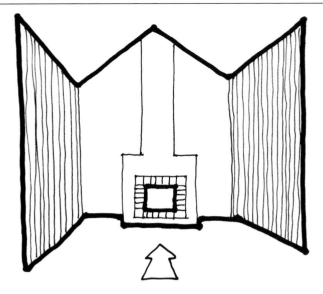

AN INTERIOR FIREPLACE BECOMES A FOCAL POINT

LAWRENCE W. SPECK

LAWRENCE W. SPECK

PB   DICK CLARK ARCHITECTURE

GLASSMAN, SHOEMAKE, MALDONADO ARCHITECTS

The size of the fireplace and the geometry of the chimney create a secondary scale to the large scale of these interiors.

BLACK & VERNOOY, AIA

DICK CLARK ARCHITECTURE

H+H

FRANK WELCH ASSOCIATES, INC.

RGH

LAWRENCE W. SPECK

PW

TAFT ARCHITECTS

CARRIE SHOEMAKE ARCHITECT

PH

WILLIAM T. CANNADY PH

RICHARD MOGAS AND ASSOCIATES ARCHITECTS

BB

STEEPLES YESTERDAY

All the form in an early Texas church is functional, too, but in a different way.

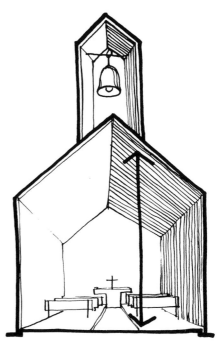

The Texas "basic" opens up full height inside. When a steeple is added, it holds the bell.

91

Without a steeple the early Texas church is a simple volumetric form.

This steeple is placed in front of the church form and is therefore the major form.

Here the steeple is set on top of the basic form of the church and is secondary to it.

Or the steeple is set at the corner of the basic church.

Pioneer Texas churches had a simple program. They were a place to worship, generally in a rectangular nave building, and they often boasted a special feature (a steeple to say *church* from a distance).

PH CHARLES TAPLEY

STEEPLES TODAY

Today the program for churches, synagogues, and temples has changed. They are community centers, with lots of places to gather beyond worship.

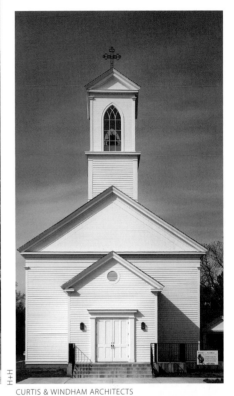

H+H

CURTIS & WINDHAM ARCHITECTS

MH HEIMSATH ARCHITECTS

There is much more than a steeple to designate their special place in the community. What hasn't changed is the role of geometry in defining houses of worship today.

Strong geometric forms define the exterior of these buildings and suggest that something special happens here.

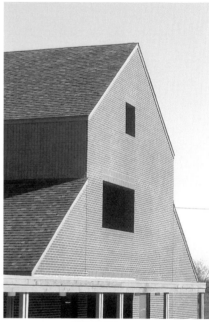

GOOD, FULTON & FARRELL ARCHITECTS

FORD POWELL AND CARSON, INC.

GOOD, FULTON & FARRELL ARCHITECTS

PH
LWK

PH   CHARLES TAPLEY

97

In places of worship, geometry is in the details as well as in the massing.

HEIMSATH ARCHITECTS   MH

HEIMSATH ARCHITECTS   MH

HEIMSATH ARCHITECTS

Interiors have a rhythm created by the structural members. Note that the light sources enhancing the forms are geometric openings in the wall, while the structure is a rhythm throughout the volume. They work together.

WILLIAM T. CANNADY

PH

HEIMSATH ARCHITECTS

MH

HEIMSATH ARCHITECTS

MH

Places of worship where the
geometry of the structure
defines the space

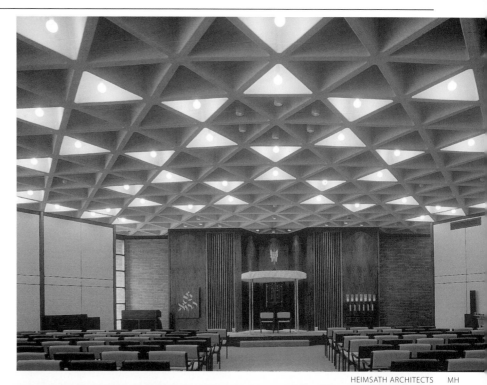

HEIMSATH ARCHITECTS   MH

FORD, POWELL AND CARSON, INC.

MATERIALS

MATERIALS YESTERDAY

The early Texas builder had only simple materials to build shelter for family and animals.

Trees for wood.

Mud for stucco.

Rocks for walls.

The pioneer Texas builder did not have the luxury of complicated buildings. The buildings had to be built from materials close at hand, with structures that were easy to construct, and with details easily assembled.

Most often the house or barn is
built of wood.

The earliest buildings are log
structures.

MH

MH

MH

Half-timber bracing is used
to reinforce the walls.

Some buildings are built with
solid stone walls which support
the roof rafters above.

Board and batten siding, often of
cedar or cypress, does not need
paint to withstand the weather.

It's the form that really counts in architecture. Decoration buzzes around the form to dress it up.

MH

MH

MH

107

Sometimes material and form coexist.

HISTORIC BUILDING

HEIMSATH ARCHITECTS

GLASSMAN, SHOEMAKE, MALDONADO ARCHITECTS

MATERIALS TODAY

Today materials can be shipped from great distances, there are many new ways of building in concrete and steel, and there are thousands of details available from a thousand catalogues.

Today an architect chooses to keep the building palette uncomplicated, and in so doing continues the integrity of the pioneer Texas tradition.

Stone and wood from the land has a special validity today, as it did yesterday.

Materials can follow the tradition of pioneer building closely or express a building in a more contemporary way.

LAKE/FLATO ARCHITECTS, INC.

RICHARD MOGAS AND ASSOCIATES ARCHITECTS

TAFT ARCHITECTS

In the example above the nearly
ruined barn became a home.

The geometry of buildings is enhanced when materials are part of the geometric composition.

Materials can add richness to a composition or they can be the skin that expresses the geometry, as shown by the white floor and walls of the interior to the right.

When materials are used as an integral part of the composition, they have design integrity.

H+H   CARLOS JIMÉNEZ

H+H

LAKE/FLATO ARCHITECTS, INC.

STRUCTURE TODAY

Today there are options. Pioneer Texas buildings can be picked up and moved.

MH

H+H
HARDAWAY/FOWLER

Buildings can be framed in wood today as yesterday.

FW
FRANK WELCH ASSOCIATES, INC.

H+H
HARDAWAY/FOWLER

Laminated wood can introduce
additional geometric forms.

The variety of images is the opportunity today. A house can be rebuilt around an original log cabin, or industrial structural components can define outdoor and indoor living spaces.

RHOTENBERRY WELLEN ARCHITECTS

HEIMSATH ARCHITECTS

LAKE/FLATO ARCHITECTS, INC.

The variety of spanning
structures today in wood, steel,
or a combination of the two
gives interiors an enviable
rhythm.

FRANK WELCH ASSOCIATES, INC.

HEIMSATH ARCHITECTS

LAKE/FLATO ARCHITECTS, INC.

H+H

BLACK & VERNOOY, AIA   B&V

H+H

RHOTENBERRY WELLEN ARCHITECTS

H+H

FRANK WELCH ASSOCIATES, INC.

B&V

BLACK & VERNOOY, AIA

H+H

LAKE/FLATO ARCHITECTS, INC.

H+H

NATALYE APPEL + ASSOCIATES ARCHITECTS, INC.

MH

HEIMSATH ARCHITECTS

DETAILS TODAY

With today's materials the architect has an expanded opportunity to enhance the geometry of the major volume with geometric details at a smaller scale.

Note that the buildings shown all use the geometric scale of details to enhance the overall geometry of the form.

In today's architecture there is celebration of details for shading.

RHOTENBERRY WELLEN ARCHITECTS

EMILY LITTLE ARCHITECTS, INC.

LAKE/FLATO ARCHITECTS, INC.

JIM WILSON ARCHITECTS

OVERLAND PARTNERS, INC.

LAKE/FLATO ARCHITECTS, INC.   H+H

MICHAEL G. IMBER ARCHITECT

WILLIAM F. STERN ASSOCIATES

JIM WILSON ARCHITECTS

LAKE   LAKE/FLATO ARCHITECTS, INC.

CURTIS & WINDHAM ARCHITECTS

Details and form coexist. Details
enhance basic design elements as
well. Note the curved stair rail
set against the rectangular exterior curtain wall.

MAX LEVY

CARLOS JIMÉNEZ   H+H

MAX LEVY

OVERLAND PARTNERS, INC.

LAKE/FLATO ARCHITECT,S, INC.

Today rehabilitation of existing buildings is widely applauded. The architects achieve a high degree of finish by reinterpreting the structure or celebrating the bold geometry of the exterior.

BLACK & VERNOOY, AIA

BLACK & VERNOOY, AIA

SHEFELMAN & NIX ARCHITECTS

BARNS YESTERDAY

The same shapes are used for

people in houses,

animals in barns.

Barns are simple geometries
made up of solids and voids. The
arch form is natural to masonry,
for it carries the weight of the
wall across the opening.

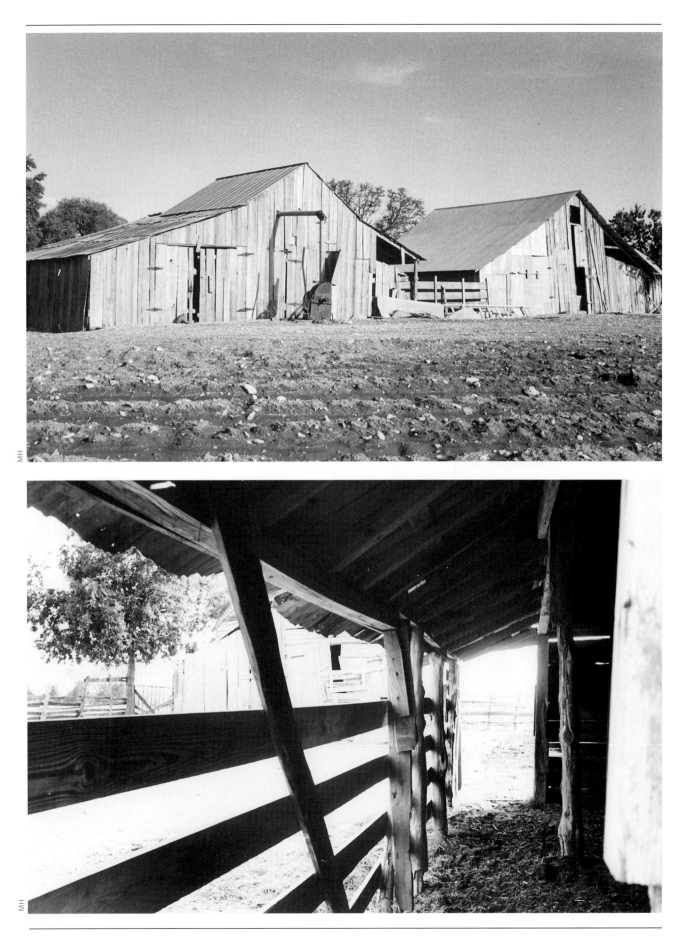

PB

DICK CLARK ARCHITECTURE

PB

DICK CLARK ARCHITECTURE

H+H   ROBERT EMMOTT

BARNS TODAY

Much has changed in Texas, but the barn has the same function today as it did in pioneer times. It makes sense that barns today continue the clear functional geometries of yesterday.

LAKE/FLATO ARCHITECTS, INC.

CURTIS WINDHAM ARCHITECTS   H+H

HESTER + HARDAWAY

LAKE/FLATO ARCHITECTS, INC.

BUILDINGS TOGETHER YESTERDAY

A house and barns make a farm.

MH

MH

MH

MH

MH

MH

MH

MH

Many houses make a town.

STORES

Stores are in towns.

Rectangles face the street, sheds cover the entrance, and the glass opens up the inside. There is still a triangular roof on a rectangular base. Some stores have false fronts to make them look bigger.

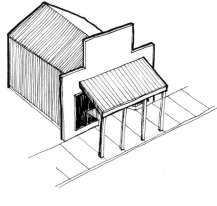

Many Texas stores are brick.

The brick arch is structural.

The decoration of the brick
fronts gives them identity.

MH

MH

MH   COMFORT, TEXAS, STREETSCAPE

H+H

JIM WILSON ARCHITECTS

BUILDINGS TOGETHER TODAY

The program for buildings together has changed over the years, but the delight of viewing related volumes has not. In pioneer years the major composition was the farm.

RG

FORD, POWELL, AND CARSON, INC.

FPC

FORD, POWELL AND CARSON, INC.

Today variety in forms suggests diverse programs, from a metro stop (see page 156) to a renovated farm site. The exciting visual fact is that simple geometric forms work today as they did in pioneer Texas times!

HEIMSATH FARM

HESTER + HARDAWAY SPREAD

HEIMSATH FARM   H+H

PTP CROSLIN AND ASSOCIATES, INC.

PH WILLIAM T. CANNADY

H+H FRANK WELCH ASSOCIATES, INC.

FW

FRANK WELCH ASSOCIATES, INC.

H+H   LAKE/FLATO ARCHITECTS, INC.

JP

PHILLIPS/WILD DESIGN

H+H

JIM WILSON ARCHITECTS